WRITING ART.

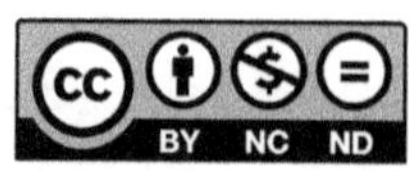

Printed by Lightning Source, Milton Keynes
in an endless edition (version 151126)
ISBN 978-94-91914-05-8

Uitgeverij, Den Haag
Shtëpia Botuese, Tiranë
出版社, Singapore

www.uitgeverij.cc

JEREMY FERNANDO,

Writing Art.

WITH AN INTRODUCTION IN ITALIAN
BY ALESSANDRO DE FRANCESCO.

:

La teoria come pratica artistica

A voler giocare con le parole e le lingue, nello spirito della Casa editrice che ospita questo volume di Jeremy Fernando — che mi ha proposto per l'appunto di redigere in italiano questa introduzione a un libro scritto in inglese —, mi viene da fare una vecchia battuta: questi saggi non sono particolarmente saggi. La loro freschezza, la loro leggerezza, l'interazione continua tra i registri linguistici, la provenienza eterogenea delle citazioni, la coraggiosa disposizione tipografica dei concetti, l'uso di colori nel testo, la brevità e talvolta l'inconclusione di stampo decostruzionista, tutto ciò contribuisce a fare di questo libro un vero e proprio ibrido teorico, una discesa ripida nel pensiero, scomoda e scorrevole allo stesso tempo.

Nello stesso spirito, direi che questi saggi sono invece dei veri "essais" nel senso originario, montaignano, della parola: dei tentativi, delle prove teoriche e formali, delle forme di apprendimento, delle esplorazioni a metà strada tra filosofia e creazione letteraria. Inoltre, questi saggi sono delle finestre aperte e spesso non richiuse su concetti che ruotano attorno ad un polo centrale, tanto ampio quanto molteplice: la creazione artistica. Jeremy Fernando, per ruotare attorno a questo polo centrale, sceglie di produrre lui stesso un pensiero mutevole, oscillante, mobile, e di assumerne le conseguenze formali come scrittore, adottando una serie di soluzioni testuali ed argomentative che ci permettono di situare questi "tentativi" all'interno di una tendenza crescente, e di crescente importanza, nel panorama filosofico contemporaneo, una tendenza che potremmo definire "pratica teorica", o "creazione teorica", ma anche, corrispettivamente, "teoria pratica" o "creativa".

È sotto un tale angolo di apertura che quest'opera dev'essere letta ed intesa. Se da un lato Derrida, Cixous, Deleuze e il pensiero francese in generale, sul quale Fernando si appoggia sovente e dal quale chiaramente proviene, ci hanno abituati ad estendere e ad aggiornare le coordinate testuali e formali della filosofia, d'altro lato questo volume è un'opera del 21mo secolo, e in quanto tale un'opera di creazione teorica, nel senso contemporaneo del termine, cosciente di essere tale, nella quale l'autore ci invita ad entrare frontalmente e senza preconcetti. Cosí, in una riflessione sulla fotografia e sulla rappresentazione come quella del primo saggio, "On Writing Light", il pensiero di Jean Baudrillard può essere altrettanto importante quanto quello del gruppo funk-rock americano Red Hot Chili Peppers, da cui Fernando cita un notevole verso, fondamentale per intuire il carattere discretamente e talvolta quasi segretamente politico del suo pensiero, in particolare quando esso è volto a criticare la debordiana ed oggi debordante *société du spectacle*: "Space may be the final frontier but it's made in a Hollywood basement". Ma gli esempi si moltiplicano: Kierkegaard e Marilyn Manson, Otis Redding in una riflessione su Beckett, e cosí via.

La pratica citazionistica di Fernando sorpassa in generale il semplice riferimento di sostegno all'argomentazione: le citazioni, nella loro eterogeneità e nella loro frequenza, spesso proposte una dopo l'altra o tipograficamente ingrandite per occupare intere pagine, sono qui dei veri e propri personaggi nella vicenda teorica dell'autore, dei microtesti *à part entière* o ancora degli ipotesti riportati in superficie. L'eterogeneità citazionistica, insieme con la libertà stilistica dell'argomentazione e con soluzioni come quella dell'uso del colore fucsia nel testo (in un saggio, l'ultimo, sostituito dal rosso), fanno pensare, *mutatis mutandis,* a quel "cozzare dell'aulico col prosaico" che Eugenio Montale vedeva, a partire da Guido Gozzano, come una delle linee evolutive della poesia italiana del Novecento.

Noto en passant che, infastidito dal carattere kitsch (Nanni Moretti mi griderebbe qui: "ma come parlaaaaa?!") del fucsia, ho chiesto spiegazioni all'autore, che si è limitato a farmi capire che il fucsia è per lui segno di positività e di gioia. Di umore piú malinconico e contrario a derive troppo kitsch ("ma come parlaaaaa?!") - fossero anche, come spero, al secondo grado - avrei preferito, per la gioia, del testo in turchese o verde smeraldo, ma non c'è stato niente da fare.

Ma vediamo piú da vicino gli argomenti dei saggi, o piuttosto quanto vorrei estrapolarne per mettere in valore ciò che di essi mi preme ed orientare allo stesso tempo il lettore verso l'esperienza di questo libro.

"On Writing Light", già citato, riprende sin dal titolo l'origine etimologica della parola "fotografia" come "scrittura di luce" e confronta la scrittura alla fotografia per una riflessione sulla visione volta ed emanciparsi dalle leggi della rappresentazione.

"On Love and Poetry" contribuisce a riabilitare la riflessione filosofica sulla poesia e ad approfondire la questione della paura filosofica della poesia di stampo platonico. In questo saggio, tra i piú lunghi, la riflessione sulla rivalità tra filosofia e poesia porta Fernando ad un'inattesa digressione sull'amore e parallelamente - sulla falsariga di Avital Ronell, il cui pensiero riappare in tutto il libro - sulla comunicazione e l'interpretazione. In altri termini, per Fernando "cosa significa amare la poesia" e "su quali basi filosofia e poesia possono comunicare" non sono domande che possono essere poste senza interrogarsi filosoficamente sull'amore e sulla comunicazione tout court.

"On Silent Songs" parte dall'opera dell'artista Charles Lim per proseguire la riflessione sul rapporto tra parola, suono e visione, scrittura e arti visive, un parallelismo assolutamente portante in tutto il libro. Ritorna qui, come già in "On Love and Poetry", la riflessione che Fernando dedica ad una delle sue opere piú care, *En attendant Godot.* Il tema dell'aspettare, e della domanda sull'identità di colui che viene atteso, sono messi da Fernando in relazione diretta, da un lato, con il ruolo della filosofia come saggezza dell'attesa, e, dall'altro, con la presenza muta dell'opera d'arte e il rapporto di osservazione come attesa dell'opera che con essa può essere costruito.

"On Playing", brillantemente costruito con proposizioni numerate come nell'*Etica* di Spinoza e nel *Tractatus* di Wittgenstein (ma anche come in ∈ di Jacques Roubaud), contribuisce, nell'economia del libro e tenendo conto dei riferimenti piú ricorrenti nel pensiero di Fernando, a ridurre la separazione tra Wittgenstein e il pensiero continentale, attraverso una riflessione sullo statuto del gioco. Ciò che interessa Fernando in questa sede è la relazione tra le regole del gioco (e l'opera d'arte come gioco) e il modo in cui queste possono essere trasgredite, sia dall'interno del gioco che a partire invece da presupposti esterni ad esso.

"I Had Some Dreams" affronta nuovamente la questione del silenzio e della comunicazione in arte, già esplorata in parte in "On Silent Songs", qui messa in relazione con quella del sogno, annunciata non solo dal titolo ma anche dall'esergo bretoniano, e con l'arte cinematografica, a partire dal lavoro di Tan Chui Mui, che Fernando rimette in scena non soltanto proponendone alcuni fotogrammi ma anche attraverso delle parti di dialogo quasi socratico tra i personaggi "beautiful loser" e "the girl", cosí chiamati, in minuscolo, quasi fossero allo stesso tempo dei nicknames in un thread di un blog. La tesi di fondo di Fernando, fortemente originale, è che un film è sempre muto, anche quando è sonoro, anche quando i suoi personaggi dialogano tra loro, perché il film parla sempre a se stesso, non avendo un interlocutore attivo e rimanendo il linguaggio e il suono in esso contenuti all'interno del dispositivo cinematografico.

"A Tryptich to — T" torna sulla fotografia e sulla questione del rapporto tra visione e scrittura in arte come modalità di interrogazione sullo statuto della rappresentazione. Qui appare per la prima volta l'uso del colore fucsia nel testo, in questo caso volto ad evidenziare delle citazioni tratte da un libro sull'hula hoop.

"Dreams of Hope", sicuramente uno dei saggi filosoficamente piú ricchi, è dedicato a Jean Baudrillard, che viene citato, ovviamente, per mezzo del colore fucsia ("ma come paralaaaa?!"). Qui Fernando riprende uno dei temi principali del suo pensiero: dalla morte dell'autore barthesiana e dalla riduzione del soggetto autoriale nella letteratura moderna, Fernando vede la scrittura essa stessa come morte (*Writing Death* è il titolo di un suo precedente libro pubblicato ivi), o meglio come vita del testo scaturente dalla morte dell'autore, vita generata dal carattere propriamente ironico (e, aggiungerei, asintotico) di questa morte. Cosí il titolo "Dreams of Hope" si trasforma, alla fine del saggio, in un "hopeless dreams" che viene reso dall'ingrandimento tipografico un vero e proprio "contro-titolo" speculare.

"Sketching in White Ink", il saggio conclusivo, è dedicato all'opera visiva e grafica di Yanyun Chen, spesso collaboratrice e art director nei progetti di Fernando. L'autore si interessa qui alla soluzione della "linea", ricorrente nell'opera grafica dell'artista, da intendersi anche come mobile linea di confine tra scrivere e disegnare. Il titolo, chiaramente iconoclasta, è una cassa di risonanza di questa tesi, che Fernando fa risalire all'incontro etimologico e gestuale tra "scratching" e *scribere,* da intendersi come sottrazione di materia anziché aggiunta, perciò come negazione della materia e della visione al momento stesso della costruzione del senso. Una vera e propria "cecità", secondo le parole dello stesso Fernando, comune al disegno e alla scrittura.

Forse è per questo che l'autore ha scelto di pubblicare questo saggio in conclusione, perché in esso viene ripreso ed esplicitato un tema ricorrente, a mio avviso il piú significativo, di tutta la raccolta: quello dell'incontro, se non di un'identità asintotica, tra le arti audiovisive e le arti letterarie. Come se nell'epoca della *société du spectacle* l'immagine potesse sperare attraverso la scrittura, e in particolare la scrittura poetica, di affrancarsi dalla rappresentazione. Ma anche come se la filosofia, per continuare —se è vero come è stato detto che la filosofia della modernità è sempre riflessione sulla possibilità della filosofia stessa —non potesse ancora una volta fare a meno dell'arte e della poesia. In questo senso, anche, Jeremy Fernando, *essayiste* del contemporaneo, pensa e realizza una teoria che è allo stesso tempo una pratica artistica. La teoria è dunque pratica dell'arte, nel senso che pratica l'arte, la attraversa, la frequenta, la rilancia e la riattiva nel reale, e pratica artistica, perché diviene essa stessa, nel momento in cui riflette, oggi, sul suo possibile—e il tema del possibile, fondamentale, è anch'esso ricorrente nel lavoro di Fernando—, una forma d'arte.

—Alessandro De Francesco

On Writing Light—

One is photographable, 'photogenic', and this is perhaps the catastrophe, that one can be photographable, that one can be captured and caught in time ...
—Hubertus von Amelunxen in conversation with Jacques Derrida and Michael Wetzel, *Copy, Archive, Signature: A conversation on Photography*

Keeping in mind that this is a conversation, an opening of possibilities with another. Not just that each photograph is an attempt to interact—allowing all echoes of *inter-* to resound with us here—with something, someone, some other; nor even that these collections are speaking with each other, in their particular sequences, within their own syntax, their own orderings, orders; but that photography itself is a conversation.

An interplay—

Between light and writing.

A writing of light.

Which opens the question: *what is being written?* For, it is not as if one can see light as such — one can only experience a certain spectrum of it, a part of it. So, even as we can see the photographs, read, have a phenomenal involvement of and with them, the question of *the status of the writing of light as a phenomenon* remains.

Not the phenomenon that stands, comes, before, the photograph. For, we should try not to forget that there has to be something before the camera, lens, film — even in a digital age where this something, this thing that stands before the photograph (whether we can still call it photography is another question), might lie in one's imagination, might reside in the imaginary (even then, there has to be something, some thing, that comes to mind before being inscribed into any photograph). And when we speak of the inscription within digital photography (perhaps we should momentarily settle for that term, that name) we should keep in mind that the digital brings with it echoes of hands, fingers (*digit*). So, it might well be a writing of light through the hand; a handful of light, perhaps even entailing a light touch.

Nor the phenomenon that is the photograph: that is clearly in front of one.

But rather, what if one sees *what light has written* rather than a writing of light? Which opens the possibility that there are two hands involved — the one holding the apparatus, and that of light. And this might well be why (s)he is called a photographer; a writer of light. Not because (s)he is the one doing the writing — after all, it is light that is writing. Which is not to say (s)he is completely divorced from the process — without her hand, light would not be able to inscribe. But that at the moment of writing, at the point where light writes, (s)he and light itself are indistinguishable.

Which means — since one cannot see light — that at the moment of photography, (s)he is blind to what (s)he is writing.

And if that is so, this also suggests (s)he not only cannot quite tell exactly what (s)he is writing, nor the outcome of that writing but, more importantly, (s)he may never be able to know if the writing, if what is written by light, is her very self.

...

The question remains: *what do we see, what are we seeing?*

For, now that we have opened the possibility that it is light that is doing the writing, writing itself as it is writing, perhaps even writing her — the hand holding the camera — as it is writing, we have to open the register that what we see is not the trace of the light, the remainder as it were, but what it is not, the *not-light* (which is not darkness, not an antonym of light) that is being written. And this brings us back to the question of sight, of seeing. For, if a *not-light,* how do we then even begin to see? Which is not even a question of what light is — even as that might well come with it — but, more pertinently, how can one speak of the negative of something we cannot quite see. Not forgetting that it is also light that we need to even begin to see. Which suggests that sight, seeing, lies within the play between light and *not-light.*

Perhaps then, seeing, sight itself, lies in the *not-.*

And more pertinently, that the *not-,* what is written by light, might well be the very one attempting to take the photograph in the first place.

...

> *The photographic image is the purest image because it does not simulate time or movement and abides by the most rigorous irrealism. All other forms of the image (cinema, video, computer-generated, etc.) are only diluted forms of the pure image and its break with reality.*
> — Jean Baudrillard

> *Space may be the final frontier but it's made in a Hollywood basement.*
> — Red Hot Chili Peppers

Not that we can even begin to tell what space is; for it is — by definition — naught.

A gap.

And it is in this gap that (s)he resides.

Not the (s)he that is of the world; that would be too banal. But the (s)he that might, could, might well be. A (s)he that "abides by the most rigourous irrealism."

A (s)he that is of the mirror.

Not a projection, nor an imaginary (s)he. For, if something was imagined, it would still have to be based on one's experiences, knowledge — it would still be that of the self. And that would be far too dull.

The (s)he that is in the mirror is one that remains unknown, unknowable. Perhaps, there to be seen; but always already slipping, evading, refusing to be enframed.

A (s)he that is of the *not*-.

And here, we should momentarily slow down, pause even, and attend to the dash that comes after the *not*. Keeping in mind that a '-' connects even as it keeps apart; that it opens the possibility of a relationality between something and something else, someone and another, something and someone. But even as the two are in a connection, they are never in the same space; there is always a gap in-between. But it is precisely this gap that is crucial: one can only be apart, if one is also a part of. For, “in order to touch, one must first have the space to do so.” (Jean-Luc Nancy)

So, even as the (s)he in the mirror is always already a mystery for the one standing in front of it, even as the (s)he of the mirror might be screaming ‘I will not be your mirror’, even as (s)he is the *not-* of you, (s)he is always also in a certain relation with you.

And perhaps the moment of her communion with you is when you open yourself to the possibility of being written by light.

The click of the shutter; or, the very possibility of a glimpse of the (s)he that is *not-*.

Which is not to say there is no risk involved. For, even as a dash connects, joins, brings together, one should also not forget that dashing opens the possibility of being dashed, broken, shattered.

...

> *You used to believe in written things regardless of whether they were true or false. If they were lies, their traces would one day serve as evidence that could be*

> *turned against their authors: the truth had merely been deferred ...*
> — Édouard Levé

> *Things keep their secrets.*
> — Heraclitus

Perhaps then, what is being written is that of the secret.

For, secrets lie not so much in their content but in their form as secret. Thus, the power of a secret, any secret, is in its significance, and not its signification. Which suggests that not only can a secret be staring one in the face — hiding in plain view — but, more importantly, that to know something is a secret, one must also be able to see it for something other than its semantic meaning.

For what it is not.

Which brings us back to the very beginning, to where we — you are part of this; after all, you are seeing, looking, writing onto the image, photo even, of the text, as you are reading, responding to and with it — began. And the consideration that perhaps this is the very catastrophe, the fatal turn, that von Amelunxen speaks of: not just that the *not*- is photographed, written in light, but that what is "captured and caught in time," can only be seen — keeping in mind that light as such cannot be seen — as *what it is not,* in non-sight, in blindness.

Can only be seen as you turn away, when you *not*-see.

Which is not a deliberate blindness, a refusal to see, but a seeing that acknowledges that it is not-seeing at the same time. One which opens itself to the possibility of the not-, whilst never quite knowing if it is the writing of light or the one attempting to let light write as (s)he writes, that we might momentarily catch a glimpse of …

… like a fleeting spectre …

Click.

…

A version of this piece—'On writing light; or, mirror mirror …'—was first published in Jasmine Seah & Jennifer Koh (eds). *Inter-Views*. Singapore: Photovoice sg, 2013: n.p.

On Love and Poetry—

or, where philosophers fear to tread

"My"—what does this word designate?
Not what belongs to me,
but what I belong to,
what contains my whole being,
which is mine insofar as I belong to it.
— Søren Kierkegaard

I can't sleep till I devour you ...
... And I'll love you, if you let me ...
— Marilyn Manson

The role of poetry in the relationalities between people has a long history — from epic poetry recounting tales of yore; to emotive lyric poetry; to rude, irreverent limericks; to Hallmark cards which have ditties that allow one to cringe and somehow fall in love at the same time, in the same moment. Without going into a notion of aesthetics, or attempting to choose which form of poetry is superior, we might want to consider why the form of poetry itself has long been a part of relationality.

And whilst doing so, we might keep in mind that poetry — especially poetry that moves, transports, us — is the form that Plato has been warning us about; particularly if we want to become good citizens.

... the poet, irremediably split between exaltation and vulgarity, between the autonomy that produces the concept within intuition and the foolish earthly being, functions as a contaminant for philosophy—a being who at least since Plato, has been trying to read and master an eviction notice served by philosophy. The poet as genius continues to threaten and fascinate, menacing the philosopher with the beyond of knowledge. Philosophy cringes ...
— Avital Ronell, *Stupidity*

And considering the notion that the philosopher is the lover of wisdom, we might begin to ask ourselves why one lover is warning against another — if the philosopher is in love with wisdom, then is the poet perhaps his rival, his challenger, for that very love? For, one must also remember that Plato — through Socrates — constantly mentions Homer as his favourite. Moreover, by adopting both his own voice, whilst mixing it with Socrates', Plato is adopting the form of poetry that he warns most about:

prosopopoeia.

A warning that almost serves more as a homage to poetry than anything else.

Here, we might open the register that one of the main reasons that he ejects a particular kind of poet is on the grounds of effecting effeminacy on the populace — for, good poetry moves you, affects you, transports you, shifts you beyond reason, *puts you out of your mind.* However, Plato also teaches us that rhetoric in its highest form requires divine inspiration by way of the *daemon*: this moment of divine intervention is one that seizes you — perhaps even causes you to cease — putting you *beyond yourself.* In other words, a good rhetorician must always already be open to the possibility of otherness — quite possibly the same otherness that resides in the feminine. One could also trace this back to the poet that he both loved and feared, most — Homer. Perhaps the effect of effeminacy that Homer's poetry opened is precisely the source of its power: through listening to Homer, one's body, one's *habitus* is opened to the possibility of the feminine. And here, one must remember that the source of all learning — and teaching — also lies in mimesis, in repetition, in habit. For, once the *habitus* is opened to the possibility of invasion, of intervention, of otherness, there is quite possibly no possibility of distinguishing whether the mimesis is that of reproduction, or if there is always already a productive aspect to it. And by extension, if learning cannot be controlled, the very notion of teaching itself is shifted from a master-student relationality to one where the master is potentially changed as well — the relationality between the master and the student is not only inter-changing, but one cannot even know who is teaching, or learning, at any point. All that can be said is that they are in a relationality; which means that one is ultimately unable to locate the locus of knowledge, of wisdom — the site of which Plato is attempting to convince us is the sole domain of the philosopher.

And, it is this that philosophy is cringing from.

To compound matters, philosophy is striving for wisdom; which can only come from the Gods. In other words, this is a gift that has to be bestowed on one — and, perhaps more importantly, wisdom is always already exterior to one's control and knowledge. At best, it is the role of one to recognise the gift, to answer the call as it were. Here, if we listen carefully, it is not too difficult to hear the echo of Alexander Graham Bell, and the telephone. And as we are attempting to respond to the call of wisdom — the call that both poetry and philosophy are listening out for — it might be helpful to recall the agreement between Alexander Graham Bell and his brother Melville.

And here, if we eves-drop on a cross-line with *The Telephone Book,* we can pick up the voice of Avital Ronell once again, and hear her teaching that:

"the connection to the other is a reading—not an interpretation, assimilation, or even a hermeneutic understanding, but a reading."

In the biography, *Alexander Graham Bell and the Conquest of Solitude,* Robert V. Bruce notes that Aleck and Melly made a "solemn compact that whichever of us should die first would endeavor to communication with the other if it were possible to do so."

Since Melville was the one who passed on first, this pact put the onus on Aleck to receive the call of his brother. If you take into consideration the fact that until Melville's death, both brothers had been working on an early prototype of the telephone, the instrument of distant sound can be read as an attempt by Aleck to maintain the possibility of keeping in touch with Melly, of hearing the voice from beyond. However, this was a connection that was not premised on any knowing, reason, or rationality; it was rather, one that was based on hope, and born out of love.

In other words, the telephone can be read as the openness to the possibility of responding to the other; one that might always remain unknown. For, even in this day of caller-identification, we can never know for sure who the other person on the line is until we pick up: hence, the only decision we can make — the effects of which we remain blind to until it affects us — is to either pick up or not, to either respond or not. And it is not as if the decision to pick up comes without risks: each time we answer a call, we run the risk of it ruining our day.

Even when we don't know whom the caller is.

Perhaps, especially when we don't know who the person on the other end of the line is.

— here one has to only think of prank calls —

And, each time we respond, pick up, we are leaving ourselves completely open to being affected by another.

...

Thus, philosophy finds itself in the position of Vladimir and Estragon.

For, since they have no idea who Godot is, they can never know if or when he shows up — thus, if he (and we are taking his gender on the word of the boy, some boy — we don't even know if it is the same boy — who comes round in the evening) has already come, they would not be in the position to know it.

And even if someone comes to them and announces that "I am Godot," the wait would not be over—without referentiality to the name, they would have to take on faith that that person is indeed Godot.

Hence, all they can know is that they are waiting for Godot; and

Godot is the name of that waiting itself.

All philosophy can know is that it is waiting; and
wisdom is the name of that waiting itself.

...

Which brings us to Tina Turner's eternal question:

"what's love got to do, got to do with it?"

And, in order to begin to consider that, we have to first attempt to examine the notion of love itself. Which might begin with an attempt to meditate on the difficult statement, *I love you.*

Keeping in mind that if love is a relationality between two persons — both of whom remain singular, whilst attempting to respond to each other — this suggests that neither of them subsume the other under themselves.

In other words, the other remains wholly other.

And, if this is so, the "you" in the statement always remains shrouded in mystery.

And, even if the "you" is replaced with the name of the person, the veiling remains: for, names refer both to the singularity that is the person, and every other person bearing that name, at exactly the same time. To compound matters, the only time one has to utter a person's name is in their absence — thus, the correspondence of a name to that particular person is at best an affect of memory. And if we are attempting to consider the notion of memory, we have to also open the register of forgetting; bringing with it the problem that there is no object to forgetting. For instance, when one utters "I forgot," all one is uttering is the fact that one has forgotten, and nothing more — the moment there is an object to the statement, one has strictly speaking remembered what one has forgotten. Moreover, one has no control over when forgetting happens to one. And since it is always already exterior to us, affects us, and has no necessary object, there is no reason to believe that every moment of memory might not bring with it a moment of forgetting. Hence, whenever we utter a name — even if we accept the correspondence between the utterance and the person in front of us — all we are doing is uttering the fact that we are naming. Thus, it is not so much that 'a rose by any other name would smell as sweet' but more appropriately, 'a rose is a rose is a rose' — the relationality between its name and the phenomenon of its sweet smell can only be established after that moment of naming, that instance of catachresis. So, whenever one utters "I love you," not only is it a performative statement, it is the very naming of that love — all you are doing is establishing a relationality between you and the other. And since there is no necessary referent — one is naming that referentiality as one utters it — this suggests that it is always already a symbolic statement; without which the mystery of the other cannot be maintained. In other words, one cannot love the other without maintaining this symbolic distance — through a ritual; in this case the utterance "I love you."

...

Which might be why Valentine's Day seems to provoke such a massive reaction: the most common one from people (besides florists) being, *Valentine's Day is mere commercialism.* Those among the nay-sayers who maintain a soft spot for Karl Marx would proceed to call it the commodification of relationships; those who prefer the Gods would claim that the sanctity of relationships has been profaned; the gender theorists would note that the expectation on males to be the gift-buyers only serves to highlight the unequal power-relation between the genders. And whichever side, variation, of the arguments chosen, their discomfort lies in the fact that they are confronted with the notion of relationships moving into a mediated sphere. Where their underlying logic is that love is between two persons only: it should not only remain between them but, more pertinently, be an unmediated experience between two.

Which, perhaps unfortunately, completely misses the point.

For, if we reopen the register that relationships are the result of a negotiation between two persons, there must then be a space between them for this very negotiation to occur. Otherwise, all that is happening is: one person is subsuming the other within their own sphere of understanding; one is effectively effacing the other. If that were the case, there would no longer be any relationality; all negotiation is gone and the other person is a mere extension of the self — one is in a masturbatory relationality with one's imaginary. Hence, any relationship must always already carry with it, within it, the unknown, and possibly always unknowable.

The other person is an enigma, remains — must remain — enigmatic.

This is perhaps the only way in which the proclamation "I love you" remains singular, remains a love that is about the person as a singular person — and not merely about the qualities of the person, what the person is. And, if the mystery of the other is unveiled, the love for the other person is then also a completely transparent love: a check-list; one that you can know thoroughly, calculate. And if they are knowable, this suggests that they can also be negated, and hence, the love can go away. Only when the love for the other person is enigmatic, one that cannot be understood, can that love potentially be an event.

And if an event, it cannot be known before it happens; at best, it can be glimpsed as it is happening, or perhaps even only realised retrospectively.

At the point in which it happens, it is a love that comes from elsewhere: this strange phenomenon is best captured in the colloquial phrase, I was struck by love; or even more so by, *I was blinded by love.* This is a blinding to not only the subject of the encounter — the self — but also of the very object of that encounter, the "you": and, all that can be said is that there is an encounter. And it is for this reason that Cupid is blind: not just because love is random (and can happen to anyone at any time) but, more importantly, because even after it happens, you remain blind to both the reason you are in love, and the person you are in love with.

Since there is an unknowable relationality with the other person, the only way you can approach it is through a ritual. This is the lesson that religions have taught us: since one is never able to phenomenally experience the God(s), one has no choice but to approach them symbolically. For, rituals are strictly speaking meaningless: the actual content is interchangeable — it is the form that is important. And it is rituals that allow us momentary glimpses at secrets; for, secrets are never about their content. Rather, secrets entail the recognition that they are secrets; the secret lies in their form as secret. This can be seen when we consider how group secrets work: since the entire group knows the secret, clearly the content of the secret is not as important as the fact that only members within the group are privy to it. Occasionally the actual content can be so trivial that even other people outside the group might know the information; they just do not realise its significance. For instance, if I used my date of birth as the password to my bank-account, merely knowing when I was born would not instantly give you the key to my life savings. In order for that to happen, you would have had to recognise the significance of the knowledge of my birthday. This means that you have to know that you know something.

And, since the God(s) are, strictly speaking, unknowable, this suggests that rituals put one in a position to potentially experience them. Which is not to say that one will necessarily — can even — know what one is experiencing. But, that one can potentially open oneself to the possibility of the experience: nothing more, and infinitely nothing less.

And it is precisely the meaningless gestures on Valentine's Day that play this role.

For, it is not so much what you give the other person, but the fact that you are giving, give, it to them. Where, the gift is very much akin to an offering — it opens the possibility of an exchange.

Remembering that gift-giving does not guarantee that you will like what is returned; for, there is always a reciprocation, but what is returned to you is never known in advance, only known at the moment it is received. This also means that the worst thing that one can do is to not give the gift: that would be akin to a cutting-off of all possibilities, a complete closing of all communication with the other. At the same time, this means that you cannot wait for the other person to give you something before you get them their gift: if that were so, the reciprocal gift would be nothing more than a calculated return. Thus, the only manner in which both persons can give true gifts is to offer them independently of the other, whilst keeping her or him in mind. In this way, the two gifts are always already both uncalculated (in the sense of not knowing what the return is) and also a reciprocation for the other (without knowing whether the other person actually has a gift in the first place). Naturally, this would seem like an irrational, even stupid, way of buying gifts. But it is precisely the stupidity involved that saves the relationship from being banal — more importantly, stupidity prevents it from entering the profane.

Which is not to say that an enigmatic love cannot end — of course it can.

However, the difference lies in the fact that if the relationality is wholly transparent, it is subsumed under reason — completely predictable, within the self, and thus never open to the possibility of otherness, exteriority, musing. A love that is an event is one that is also open to the possibility of the divine, the sacred — always already closer to the possibility of wisdom.

And, if we establish — or, at least posit — that both love and wisdom are exterior to our knowledge, and might be the finitude of our selves, this suggests that both are names for the possibility of openness to otherness. In other words, and what choice do we have here but to use the words of the other, the philosopher — the lover of wisdom — is a name for one who is waiting, and nothing more.

But that still leaves us with the question of this uncomfortable relationality between philosophy and poetry.

However, before we address that question, we might have to take a momentary detour, and consider the whether it is possible to call one, let alone one-self, a poet. For, if we take the notion of a poet to be one who reaches the highest levels of rhetoric (beyond the lawyer, and the orator, who aim to either please the crowds, or convince by way of sophistry), then we must also acknowledge that one can only become a poet at the moment one is seized, at the point one is inspired, by the *daemon*. Without this divine moment, all (s)he can do is practice her craft. And, as no one can control when the *daemon* makes its appearance, one could always be practising in vain — in some way, one is always already practising to be least in the way when the *daemon* whispers into one's ear; one is practising so as not to be vain. And since one cannot know when — or even if — the *daemon* will appear, there is no time frame to the practising: unlike the lawyer who speaks against a clock, poetry knows no time; the only time that matters is the time appropriate to poetry itself.

Thus, all the poet (if one can use this term) is practising for is the possibility of effacing her self — for the possibility that is waiting. Thus, in order for poetry to occur, in order to be seized, the poet — along with all her concerns — must cease.

In other words,

there is no poet;
only the possibility of poetry.

Sacrifice destroys that which it consecrates. It does not have to destroy as fire does; only the tie that connected the offering to the world of profitable activity is severed, but this separation has the sense of a definitive consumption; the consecrated offering cannot be restored to the real order.

— Georges Bataille, *The Accursed Share*

However, even as there is no time frame to this waiting, even as all we can say is that poetry is a name for waiting, the one who is practising is always already also in time. And since (s)he is in a symbolic relationality with the possibility of poetry, this suggests that the practising—her practise—is her sacrifice; and time is precisely what she is sacrificing.

Here, it might be helpful to turn to a strange source when it comes to poetry—Bataille—and consider his reminder that, the "essence [of sacrifice] is to consume *profitlessly*": this is where each exchange is beyond rationality, beyond calculability, beyond reason itself, "unsubordinated to the 'real' order and occupied only with the present."

Since there is no need for a physical change in the object of sacrifice—"it does not have to destroy as fire does"—this suggests that the tie is severed symbolically. Hence, there is an aspect of trans-substantiation in this sacrifice: the form remains the same; in fact there is no perceivable change — this is the point at which all phenomenology fails — but there is always already a difference, an absolute separation from the "real order," from logic, calculability, reason. The object of sacrifice, "the victim [,] is a surplus taken from the mass of *useful* wealth ... Once chosen, he is the *accursed share*, destined for violent consumption. But the curse tears him away from the order of things ..." And it is this tearing away from the order of things — the order of rationality — that "restores to the sacred world that which servile use has degraded, rendered profane." For, only when it is no longer useful, when it is no longer abstracted — subjected, subsumed under — merely a use-value, can the object be an object as such, can a subject be a subject as such; be a singularity. Thus, it is never so much who or what is sacrificed, but the fact that there is a sacrifice.

So even as (s)he is sacrificing her time to poetry, it is always already beyond her knowledge whether what (s)he is doing is actually preparing her for poetry or not — all (s)he can know is that she is sacrificing and nothing more.

Hence, all (s)he can do is to open her self to the possibility of this relationality —

all (s)he can do is be in love with poetry.

And, at the moment the muse whispers into her ear, (s)he ceases to be, and becomes a medium for poetry.

And since this possession is always already beyond our cognitive knowledge, this is also a moment of divine wisdom.

In other words, there is no difference between poetry and wisdom —

the moment of poetry is the moment of wisdom.

Where, it is not just that poetry, distant sounds, love, wisdom, are premised on relationality, but that they are perhaps relationality itself. A relationality that cannot quite, cannot even, know of itself as a relation, but is only — always already — an openness to the possibility of relationality;

that is waiting …

And this might be the very reason for the philosopher's aversion to poets. Not so much because they may corrupt the youth (this is, after all, the aim of all thinking, all philosophy), but precisely because in order to do so, the philosopher must wait for a moment of possession, for divine musing, for poetry.

Hence, all thought, all thinking, all philosophy, is nothing but the waiting for the possibility of — the possibility that is — poetry itself.

...

A version of this piece was first published in *continent: A Quarterly Review of Culture* (1:1), 2011.

On silent songs…

for Charles Lim

I

Sittin' in the mornin' sun
I'll be sittin' when the evenin' comes
Watching the ships roll in
And then I watch 'em roll away again, yeah
— Otis Redding

One does wonder who, or what, it is that rolls away — whether it is the ships that come and go, or if their arrivals, departures, were a result of my watching. Or perhaps, it was always only the waves that were bringing them back and forth. For, regardless of what the people on the ships would like to think, all their engines, machines, attempts at movement, motion, would be rather futile if the waves decided not to play along. Maybe then, it was always the waves that were moving — whilst the ships and I remained, were what remained of movement.

All I remember doing is watching, even as I was never quite sure exactly what I was watching, if I were actually the one watching—*watching the tide roll away*—or, if they were watching me.

But, it's not as if I am going anywhere. Can I even go anywhere unless someone sees me, watches me, do so?

Can I—can anyone—do anything but watch?

Wait.

Bearing in mind that waiting has no object. For, the moment one knows what, or whom, one is waiting for, waiting has ended: one is already in expectancy, where arrival is the mere actualisation, where waiting is only a phase. And, like Vladimir and Estragon, all one can do is: either leave or wait.

As I too could have decided to end waiting.

To no longer watch the tides rolling away, ships sail in. But since I could not get it out of my mind—since I could not but wonder if it were the ships that were moving, or the waves, or if it were me—thought had already seized me. And in that moment, in that inability to step away from the moment, I was also already waiting.

Not for anyone, but for a name.

At least Vladimir and Estragon were told the name of whom they were awaiting — even if Godot is nothing but the name of waiting itself.

Perhaps then, the only question I can ask is:

whom do I await?

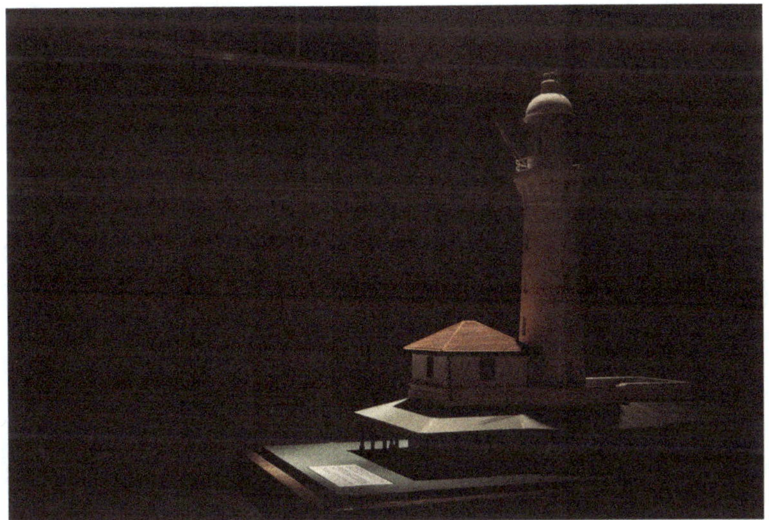

Sittin' here resting my bones
And this loneliness won't leave me alone

Or, perhaps, all I can do is name whom I am awaiting; without ever knowing who or what this name corresponds with. Which is not to say I will not expect: for, without expectations — one could also call it hope, if one prefers — is there even any waiting? Which also means: without a name, without naming, one has already stopped waiting, has already left.

Perhaps then, if I cannot yet name whom I await, I can first name myself. Which is not to say that one's name ever comes from oneself — it always already precedes one. And in saying one's own name, one might well be only echoing the name all others call one.

Not as if one can ever house light,

keep it within one.

Unless perhaps one opens the register that there might always be ghosts, spectres, hauntings, within one's haunt. And that the familiar, the familial, is often also the most strange, odd, unfa-

They call me, a

light-house.

miliar. Never forgetting that even as one might attempt to keep the light within one, it can only be seen from without.

Perhaps then, I will never know if this light from me is mine, or merely a reflection of an ancient light from Alexandria. For, even as one might not be seeing the same light, one can always hear it in what they call me: *phare; faro; farol; phari; pharos ...*

Perhaps then, trying to keep light — let alone try to keep tabs on light, to make light visible to the one from whence it came — is always already wasting time.

But, it is not as if time is ever one's, ever belongs to one. Perhaps then, all one can do is to live as if one has time — as if it were one's time, as if it were one's own time, as if one could possibly own time.

Perhaps all I can do is: name myself as I was named, as if I was naming.

And await light itself.

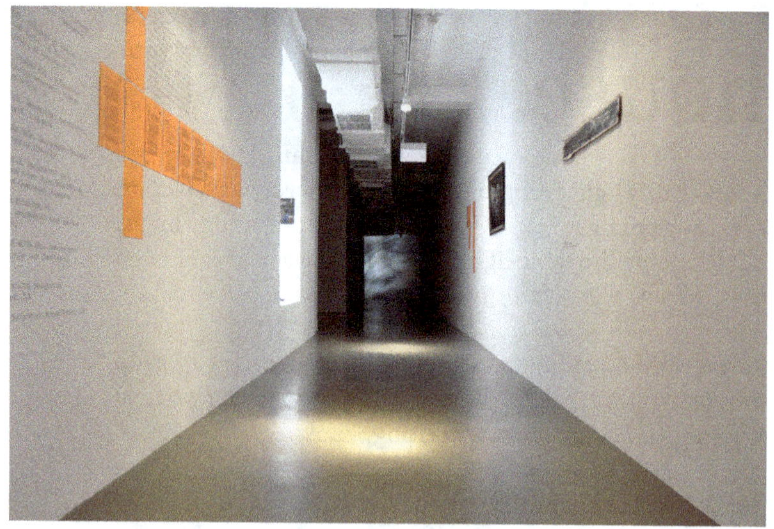

II

But what if the "work of art" is housed in a museum, placed in the haunt of the muses? Might its "act of resistance" not already be muted? For, the moment the muses are housed, are placed within an *oikos*, they also withdrawn from the *polis*, from the public. They are made *private* — never forgetting that to be private is also to be made voiceless; to be excluded from citizenry; to be the one that cannot learn; to be an *idiotēs*.

However, what saves its potentiality is: the "affinity" between the work of art and an act of resistance is a "mysterious relation." Where it can be glimpsed, sensed even, but that the exact relationship remains beyond one,

The work of art is not an instrument of communication. The work of art has nothing to do with communication. The work of art strictly does not contain the least bit of information. To the contrary, there is a fundamental affinity between the work of art and the act of resistance ... what is this mysterious relation between a work of art and an act of resistance when men who resist have neither the time nor sometimes the necessary culture to have the least relation to art?

I don't know ...

— Gilles Deleuze, 'Having an Idea in Cinema (on the Cinema of Straub-Huillet)' outside the realm of cognition, where one can perhaps only say,

I don't know.

And like all true mysteries, they also have the power — an unknown power — to make us tremble.

III

All I could see is its light.

Pointing out at me, towards me, calling out at me to rush towards it, go to it, and then ebb from it, always ebbing even whilst flowing towards it. Even as I've been told that it was never meant for me, that it was only meant for my wards, the ones that I allow to move. Even as I've been told that the light guides them, precisely by warning them away from it: a light that shines to ensure that my wards do not take a shine to the source of its shining.

As if I would not care for my own wards.

Unless, of course, they attempt to ward me off — seeking their protection from other sources, other guardians, others.

Helios for instance.

I suppose they were also trying to tame me by pretending to understand what I am, who I am. By naming me — naming as an attempt at *apotropaios*. Keeping in mind that one only needs to use a name in the absence of the object to which the name is referring to — thus, ultimately, in preparation for the death of the one that is named.

And more than that: the moment one is named, one is always also enframed — all naming involving choices, selections, pickings, as well as exclusions. In other words, once named, the manner in which one is seen, heard, understood is both opened and closed, at the same time: another that hears, sees, one's name is free to interpret one's name as (s)he chooses, but there there are rules. For, since one's name comes before one, there are always already stories that come with any name, every name.

And there is no reason that mine, I, would be any different.

And since the register of framing is opened, one must never forget that to frame something, someone, is to accuse them of something they haven't done, might not have done, at least not yet: to name them as guilty. Which is not to say that names are false — they certainly are not — but neither are they true. They just are: and remain so. Which might be their greatest crime.

In the beginning was the Word

But, it was a definite word — not any of the multitude of words that we use. It was the word beyond words; a sound. Just like the sounds of me going back and forth, ebbing and flowing.

Coming and going.

Perhaps, all that one can say, maybe even all that I can ever say, is:

I am a sound.

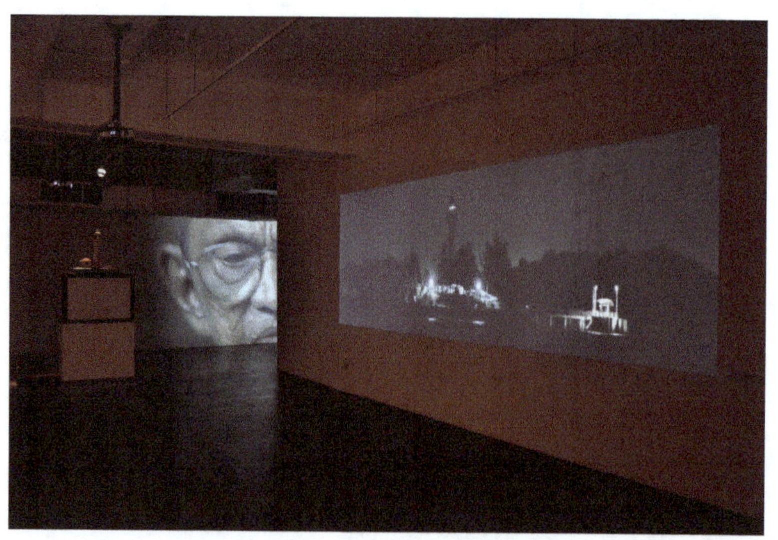

Pontus.

Two syllabi rolling air out, back in, as they are uttered. Going forth; rushing back in. Sounds that keep my wards afloat: for, even as they may be heading eventually to land, it is often sounds that draw one to shores which are the most dangerous.

Just ask Odysseus.

And even as my name is not quite a name, just a sound, two sounds, where the link between the sounds, where the movement between the one rushing out and the gentle return remains unknown, perhaps even mysterious, if one listens carefully to it — not to the name but to the sound of it, to the sound of its flow, to the silent sound in-between its turn — one might hear my soundless song to my wards.

Row row row your boat
Gently down the stream
Merrily, merrily, merrily, merrily
Life is but a dream

...

This piece was inspired by, was written as a response to, Charles Lim's In Search of Raffles' Light, which was exhibited at the National University of Singapore Museum, 24 October 2013 – 27 April 2014. All photos in this chapter are credited to Kenneth Tay & the NUS Museum.

On Playing

1. Games are to be played

1.1 There are rules in any game
1.11 One can choose to follow the rules
1.112 One can choose to break the rules
1.12 If one follows the rules one can play the game
1.121 If one does not follow the rules one cannot play
1.122 If one breaks the rules while playing, one can no longer play the game
1.2 If one wants to play, one will follow the rules
1.21 If one wants play well, one must know the rules well
1.22 Playing well means being serious about rules
1.221 Since one chooses to be serious about rules, one chooses to be serious about games
1.222 Choosing to be serious about games means choosing to be serious about play.

2 Playing seriously is playing to win

2.1 Winning involves defeating one's opponent(s)
2.11 The winner is the one that is ahead of her or his opponent(s) as deemed by the rules

2.12 One can only beat one's opponent(s) within the rules of the game

2.2 If winning requires the rules, this means that a judge has to rule in one's favour

2.21 Playing the judge is playing the game

2.22 Playing the judge is the game

3. Playing the game is playing with the rules of the game

3.1 One can only play with rules within the rules of the game

3.11 The judge is the one who decides if one is adhering to the rules or not

3.12 Playing with the rules means playing with the judge

3.2 A judge can only judge based on what (s)he sees, or hears.

3.21 Judgement is based on interpretation

3.22 Playing with the rules means playing with the interpretation of the judge

3.23 The only basis of judgement is the judge

3.231 A judge has no way of telling if (s)he is right or wrong except by judging her own judgement

3.232 If the judge can only judge when (s)he is judging, each judgement is also a judgement of the rules

3.233 If the judge can only judge when (s)he is judging, everything (s)he judges is potentially in exception to the rules

3.234 Each time the judge judges, (s)he is writing the rules of the game

3.3 The judge is the game

4. Playing is the undoing of the game

4.1 Even though the game is undone, each time one plays rules are written

4.1.1 Since the rules are recognised as rules they might well be the same rules as the ones before

4.1.2 As the rules are the game, it might well also be the same game

5. Every time one plays, one is always already re-playing

I Had Some Dreams;

or, Tan Chui Mui in my coffee…

> *As far as I am concerned, a mind's arrangement with regard to certain objects is even more important than its regard for certain arrangements of objects, these two kinds of arrangement controlling between them all forms of sensibility.*
> — André Breton

It speaks to me.

Or perhaps, I should say: her film speaks to me.

But, what does that mean, what can it possibly mean to say that? For, it is not as if films speak; nor are their filmmakers there — at the site where this alleged speaking to, speech, takes place — as one is watching the film. Even if one knows the filmmaker, even if one has watched the film because the filmmaker is a friend, even if I had spoken with Tan Chui Mui long before I had ever seen, watched, *Tanjung Malim* 有棵树 (*A Tree in Tanjung Malim*). For, even if one speaks with the one who makes the film before, or after, watching the film, even if said filmmaker gives one a running commentary as the film is played, that would be someone — granted not just any but one with an intimate relation with the moving images — speaking over the film.

The film itself remains silent.

For, what is cinema but the relationship between images moving through time and sound. And the one who watches, bears witness to this. Film speaks, not to the one who watches, but to itself.

Thus, *silent movie* is a tautology:

films are always silent.

... if one puts together a block of movements/ duration, perhaps one does cinema. It is not a matter of invoking a story or of contesting one. Everything has a story. Philosophy tells stories as well. Stories with concepts. Cinema tells stories with blocks of movement/ duration.
— Gilles Deleuze, 'Having an Idea in Cinema: on the Cinema of Straub-Huillet'

What they show, share, are their images: their sound, their speech, is for themselves alone.

And the one who watches eavesdrops.

Attempting to listen to, into, something that was never even meant for her. Perhaps what (s)he hears is not only through a transgression, via a trespass, but more importantly, might have nothing to do with the sound that is in relation with the moving pictures themselves. Not that the sound, speech, within the film is any different from the one (s)he hears, but that the speeches, sounds, (s)he hears might well only be the ones (s)he hears. For here, it might be apt to once again tune our receptors to Breton, and his reminder in *Nadja* that "time is a tease. Time is a tease because everything has to happen in its own time." And the speaking in the film — the speech of the film — occurs in its own time; a time that has naught to do with the time of the one who sees. And yet, as (s)he watches, (s)he sees in her own time, can only see in her time; quite possibly brings the sound (s)he hears into her time.

Thus, not for her and yet always only for her.

Perhaps all we hear are our "mind's arrangement with regard to certain objects" ... nothing more, and infinitely nothing less.

Perhaps then, always already,
Tanjung Malim 我有棵树
(*My Tree in Tanjung Malim*).

After all why would one think about — write about — a film unless it speaks to one? A line, an admission, that perhaps can only be uttered, admitted to, that is only permissible, in secret, as a secret.

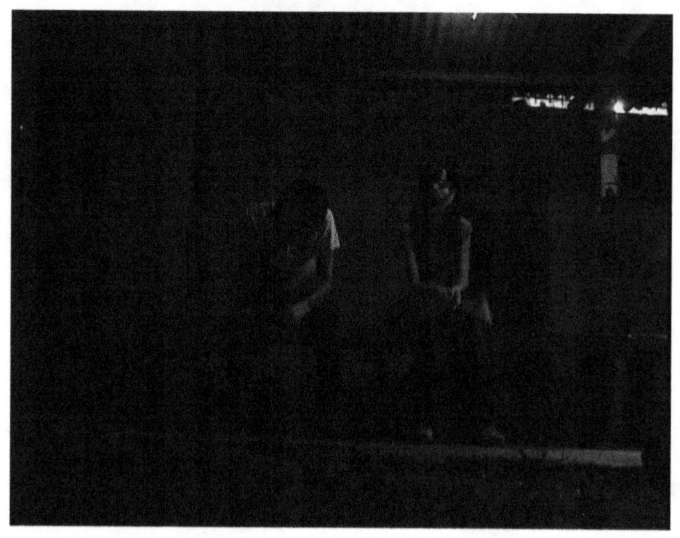

I was thinking ... Even if I failed to get to where I wanted to go ... I get to see beauty anyway.

—the girl

Mr Panda ... his biggest wish in life ... is to see a colour photograph of himself.

—beautiful loser

They speak.

Perchance to dream.

Certainly, they speak of dreams, their dreams, dreams perhaps even of themselves—"would you ever fall for me"—, speak of their dreams of having dreams.

And perhaps, as they speak, we dream of hearing them speak, of them speaking.

But since we speak of speaking, since in watching the film—in watching films—you might have heard some speech, some ones speaking, perhaps it might be time to attend to the question of: *what is it to speak?* Which is also the question of: what is it to speak *with?* For, there is no speech—or, at least, no known speech; no knowledge of there being speech—unless one is heard speaking, even if it is oneself that is hearing one speak.

Thus, to speak is to *converse,* to be in conversation.

Bearing in mind that to converse is to live with, to turn about (*vertere*) with (*con*). Which does not necessarily mean agreement: for, to converse is also to be the exact opposite. Which means that: to converse is *to be with* whilst also possibly *turning around* (*conversus*), *turning about* (*convertere*). However, even as there might be a disagreement, it is an opposition that continues to maintain the relation; maintains the poles on the same plane, as it were; that still agrees to be with, even as both are turning, moving around. That even as there might be divergences, even as one is momentarily turned away from or even against (*versus*) the other, there is always already an openness to the possibility of changing one's mind, one's position, openness to the possibility of conversion.

That, even as the beautiful loser replies in the negative to the girl's question — tells the girl to "give me a break. Take a look at yourself. You're not even grown" — this is a *no* that does not negate, that certainly does not remain certain. After all, she will grow, is growing, has already grown as his answer is being uttered. But, whether this ever happens or not is perhaps only known, can only be known, in the time of the film itself — in the conversation between the two that follows, that perhaps continues.

However, it is the *turn* in conversation — the turn in the coming together, in the *with* — that might be crucial to us.

For, even as I posit that film is silent, that the sound in films remains for the film, it is not as if we do not form a relationality with the sound that we hear, that we listen into; even if the sound is not there, even if we do not hear a sound, even if there is no speech for us to hear. And, it would be too simple — and erroneous — to say that the sound, any sound, comes from us, from the one who hears. If that were true, we would never be able to have a conversation about the speech in films, never be able to share an experience of the sound of films with another. Thus, even as we consider the possibility that the speech in film happens in its own time — and that our hearing of it occurs in our time — we might also open the dossier that it is in the turn, during the turn, that both times meet, come together, converse. That even as both might well be completely different registers — perhaps even completely opposite, oppositional, ones — they still maintain the possibility of speaking to one another.

That in that perhaps *silent speech* — silent enactment of speech; speaking that remains silent — between the sound in relation to the images and the sound we hear, there might be speech; they might be speaking with each other. A speech that perhaps occurs at the very moment where the images are moving from one to the next, turning from one to another. One that is perhaps as illusory as the very movement itself. A speech, a speaking, that might well remain beyond us. Even as we might — even as we clearly do — hear it speak.

Thus, a speech that remains silent even as we hear it. That retains a silence for itself even as it is heard. That speaks to us even as it retains its silence.

That keeps its secret from us even as we listen in, attempt to listen to it, listen in on it.

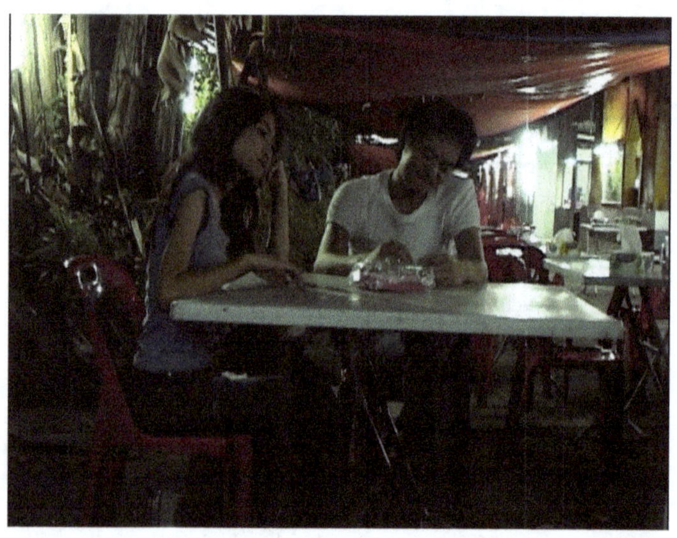

On ne voit rien. On n'entend rien. Et cependant quelque chose rayonne en silence ...

— Antoine de Saint-Exupéry

You see nothing. You hear nothing. And yet something shines, something sings in that silence ...

— *The Little Prince*, translated by Richard Howard

Secrets perhaps shine.

And, this might well be the way in which we detect — or, at least, this is possibly how we might catch a glimpse of — the secret that the sound, the speech in film, keeps for itself.

That little glimmer that calls out to us.

That is perhaps the very sound of a film that calls out — to us. Calls us forth to see, calls forth to us to look, to think, to think with it, to attend to it, be with it — if only for a moment.

For, one should try not to forget that the content of secrets rarely matter: knowing my mother's maiden name is not all that important, unless you also know that it is the password for my bank account. Thus, the power of secrets lies in the knowledge of their significance — as secrets.

Perhaps this is why everyone can hear the same sounds from, speech in, a film; hear the same silence — for, it is not as if the silence is separate from the sound, from the speaking, but that the sound brings with it its silence, is in conversation with its silence, is with (*con*) its very own opposite (*versus*) — but not notice, not attend to, its rays, its "shining."

Which is not to say that — just because one attempts to attend to these glimpses — one knows anything more than another who does not. For, the power of a secret lies in maintaining itself as a, in keeping itself, secret; even though one knows that it is one. In fact, a secret always needs a community: if only one person knows of it, it is hardly a secret — secrets have to be shared, but at the same time only by some. A shared exclusion, an exclusionary sharing. Where perhaps all that the ones in communion with, through, the secret know is that they share a secret.

Thus, even as one thinks, perhaps hopes, that one is catching a glimpse of this secret, this silence in speech — even if one is attempting to open oneself to its possibilities, open oneself to speaking with, being in communion with, conversing with, this absolute otherness that is this silence — one is always also running the risk that one might well be speaking not just with another but with oneself.

And perhaps, this is the true risk of opening oneself to this secret: that one discovers not just that there is a silence in the film that remains hidden from one's glimpse, that remains secret from one, but that there is always also potentially a silence in oneself, a silence in one to oneself.

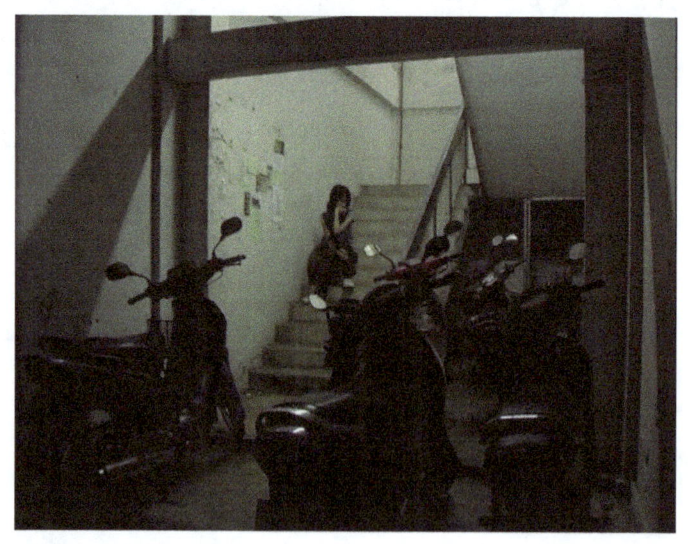

You'd already told me earlier

— beautiful loser

I missed my stop on the bus this morning. Ended up in the middle of nowhere. There was a tree by the side of the road. White flowers constantly falling ... the flowers were thin like serviette.

— the girl

Perhaps this time, it was for us.

Or, at least I'd like to think so.

And as for the calling out from the film — "Tan Chui Mui, what the hell do you know" — that, perhaps, should remain between the film and its maker.

Not that we can unhear it.

But we should resist the attempt — the pretense even — to know. For, it would have been too easy to claim that the film is alluding to autobiography, or that the film is aware of itself as film, of its making, its maker.

For, we shall — or at least attempt to — save ourselves from such banality.

And merely allow it to echo in us; an echo that allows us to remind ourselves of the possibility that as we watch, as we listen …

… no one sings me lullabies
And no one makes me close
my eyes
So I throw the windows wide
And call to you across the sky

— Pink Floyd, *Echoes*

…

This piece is dedicated to Denah Johnston & Kym Farmen, without whom, it would not have been possible. The film-stills from *A Tree in Tanjung Malim* were very kindly provided by Tan Chui Mui and Da Huang Pictures. Many thanks also to Jacky Yeap for his help in procuring the photographs. A version of this piece was first published in *Berfrois: Intellectual Jousting in the Republic of Letters*, on 27 October 2014.

A Triptych to—T

III

Poetry is not about seeing the invisible, or the very visible. Poetry, instead, is about seeing the slightly visible.
—Michel Deguy

If so, what is this glimpse that you are offering us?
An offering that perhaps remains slightly invisible to us, even as we may be catching, think we might be catching, hope to catch, a glimpse, glimpses, of it.

Keeping in mind that if a gift is a true gift—given without expectation of a particular return, is not merely strategic, performative—it may not just be something that is not liked by the one who receives it, but may not even be a thing at all.

An offering that might well remain in its being offered.

For, as Hélène Cixous never lets us forget, "when the visible has overtaken the invisible who can tell whether the visible will not allow the invisible to be seen, and that we will have eyes to lose in it." So, perhaps not just our own inability to see, but that if perhaps seen, it will no longer be invisible: that what allows it to be "slightly visible," to be poetry, is the fact that something always also, always already, remains invisible, if only slightly.

Perhaps then, only an offering as what is being offered by her remains veiled from us.

After all, I was not there when the picture was taken.

Which does not mean that her offering does not affect us. For, even as she hints at the safety of anonymity that the writer can hide behind — I have been told about the safety / of being the third person, / in a story, / in a poem, / in a song — albeit only in a parenthesis — (told that the writer need not expose her identity, / admit her tragic fantasies, / or produce her lover's particularly plosive name) — (perhaps hiding away the fact that there is no hiding away, as it were), this does not say anything about the safety of, offer any safety to, the reader, to the one who attempts to read.

For, reading — attempting to attend to — opens not so much the text, which remains veiled from us, slightly invisible, but the one who reads.

> *If you want to read, jump, do not set yourself so much as a comma.*
> — Hélène Cixous

Where the moment I grazed not, even before there, we burst
... for it is we — perhaps only me — whom it exposes.

Where reading poetry
— if I could offer my six cents —
is tautological ...

... for, **reading is poetry**

I

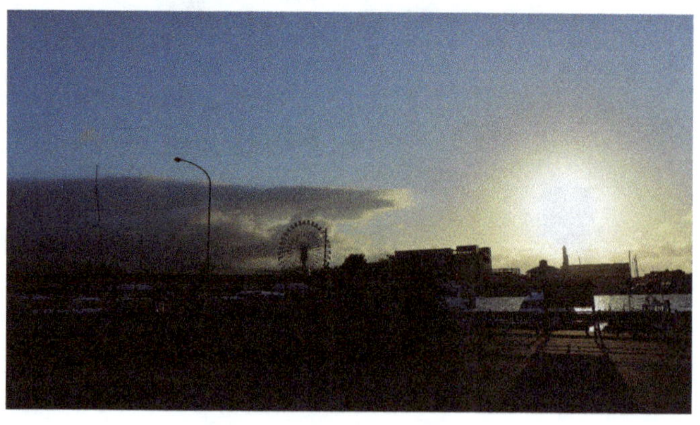

(Alice Renez Tay, 'A certain wonderland that illuminates rather than just shines ...', 2013)

II

> *To know that one does not write for the other, to know that these things I am going to write will never cause me to be loved by the one I love (the other), to know that writing compensates for nothing, sublimates nothing, that it is precisely there where you are not — this is the beginning of writing.*
> — Roland Barthes

And, it is not just that one cannot write for another, for the other; not just that writing always only points to the absence of the one that one is attempting to write about, on; that writing only marks "where you are not"; not just that the first other is the one who reads what one writes, that brings one's writing into being through reading it — keeping in mind that reading is only possible because of what remains *slightly invisible* — that the first other is oneself; but that it is only because of this impossibility that writing itself can begin. And more precisely — even as precision itself might well be ironic, perhaps even absurd, here — impossible because what remains *slightly invisible* is, whether one has written or not: not in the sense of whether there is a mark, but whether the mark is from one, or from "where you are not."

Thus, not just that "one does not write for the other," but that in writing, the one who writes might well be the other, another.

Hence, there is quite possibly no writer — only writing.

Which might be why it is only he — through T — that could give us, the young ones, classes on how to draw, to write:

First, draw a leaf. Start from nature.
Fill in the veins. Or, a hand. The smooth and
Subtle forking lines. Next, definite shapes such as
a cube, a ball. The human form comes last.
And before that, objects upon objects.
Translate vision into prose, then brushstrokes,
until it is one with the other. As in life,
allow impreciseness. Attend to colour,
to suggestion.

But, even as what appears in front of us might be drawing, writing, we might try not to forget — perhaps all this is but splattered ink on paper,/ all smudges and blots.

Words are foolish, they signify nothing.
They sing.

Which opens the question of: how can we, one, read when one cannot quite be sure of what lies in front of us, if what is in front of us might well be lies? If all might just be *sound and fury*. Or perhaps, a sort of paper marked with memories.

Perhaps then, also a question of legibility, visibility.
And, the question of, as Cixous might say, "can the illegible be legible?"

Moi je laisserais tomber
mais le livre ne veut pas.
— Hélène Cixous

Nous sommes à la merci de la
volonté de nos livres.
— Daniel Chan

Même si, peut-être surtout parce que, nous à lisons l'aveuglette.

But perhaps, reading blindly is precisely what allows us to listen, opens the possibility of listening — to the song of the words, the whispers of what remains slightly invisible, as they sing. Which might be why some part of me wishes that

I had seen, been able to see, her notes: for, all of the notes might well have been speaking in, might well sing in, their own notes.

Had been able to listen to T

— to the rhythm of the words —

music

But, since one never quite knows, can know, if one is *listening to* what is slightly invisible, or if they are only *sounds in one's head,* this means that all reading — even if, perhaps especially if, reading is an attempt to respond to what is not quite there — is both a *listening to* and also a *singing along with.*

Perhaps then, the only response to her gift, to Tamara's gift, is to offer — not in return, but alongside hers — a song:

- *Go to your record cabinet*
- *Pull out Nina Simone's 'I Wish I Knew How It Would Feel To Be Free'*
- *Play*

One to listen to,
whilst playing with a hula hoop

... in the shadow of a *date tree.*

...

All lines in pink have been read from, can be read in Tammy Ho Lai-Ming. *hula hooping*. Hong Kong: Chameleon Press, 2015.

But what could art possibly mean in a world that has already become hyperrealist, cool, transparent, marketable? All it can do is make a final, paradoxical wink — the wink of reality laughing at itself in its most hyperrealist form ... irony.

Yet this irony itself is no longer part of the accursed share. It now belongs to insider trading, the shameful and hidden complicity binding the artist who uses his or her aura of derision against the bewildered and doubtful masses.

Irony is also part of the conspiracy of art.

... and what hope have we
when irony has been taken from us?

For, what else is irony but a gap — a space-between. And what else is space but the very condition of art itself;
— space — which opens
the possibility for us to be
living with art.

Not just material space, the
space of materiality.

But that of imagination;
the very place of
possibilities.

The space for the work to be — maybe even to breathe. Not in the way in which one wants, you want, it to be, but in the manner in which it is. And perhaps, at some point, if you are quiet enough, attentive enough — if one opens oneself to the work — it might whisper to you.

Might call out to you.
Which means that one's role — one's choice — is to either pick up or not.

Not that one can ever know if one is answering a call from another, from the work, or if all one is hearing, if all you are hearing, are merely *voices in your head ...*

Why is the call thought of as something which, rather than taken, taken down, or taken in — be it from a specific agent, subject, principle, preferably a moral one — will be given? And if each call which issues is destined to make demands on the one who is called (but this is also questionable), is it already settled that I will hear, that I will hear this call and hear it as one destined for me? Is it not rather the case that the minimal condition to be able to hear something as something lies in my comprehending it neither as destined for me nor as somehow oriented toward someone else? Because I would not need to hear it in the first place if the source and destination of the call, of the call as call, were already certain and determined. Following the logic of calling up, of the call ... and along with that the logic of demand, of obligation, of law, no call can reach its addressee simply as itself, and each hearing is consummated in the realm of the possibility not so much of hearing as being able to listen up by ceasing to hear. Hearing ceases. It listens to a noise, a sound, a call; and so hearing always ceases hearing, because it could not let itself be determined other than as hearing, to hearing any further. Hearing ceases. Always. Listen ...

— Werner Hamacher

Which suggests that one cannot quite know what it says to one — nor, if it is even saying anything to one — at least with any certainty.

And here, what has to be resisted is the attempt to explain, to rationalise; to put whatever what thinks one might have heard — from the call — back under one's schema, schematics, heuristics, back under rationality itself. For, it is often easier to rely on reason — no matter how fictive — than to not have anything to cling onto. Which might be why conspiracy theories are so popular: underlying them is the logic that someone — no matter how implausible — is in control. Whether the reasons given are true or not are perhaps irrelevant: the fact of there being a reason, a cause, is better than if there were none. In many ways, it is even better if the reason is fictional: for, if grounded in a certain fact, or reality, it can then go away. However, if it is in the realm of the imagination, it is then always already possibly independent from materiality: thus, can be applied to any and every situation. And it is this, to echo Friedrich Nietzsche, that gives us us the metaphysical comfort that we can know — can dream we know — what is going on.

But to do so, is to do nothing other than to break the relationality, the connection — to close all possibilities of the call itself. For, if subsumed, comprehended, it is also seized, grasped, apprehended; quite possibility torn apart.

Here, one should never forget — or at least try never to forget — the teaching of Jean Baudrillard: explication, attempts to explain, analysis, only break apart [*ana* 'up, throughout' + *lysis* 'a loosening,' from *lyein* 'to unfasten']. And, if beauty is of the order of the whole, the complete — even if this remains in the imaginary, as an idea, in the realm of the *eidos* — any attempt to analyse can only, at least might only, worsen. For art, like the poem, lacks nothing: any commentary makes it worse. Not only does it lack nothing, but it makes any other discourse look superfluous.

However, it is not as if opening oneself to the possibility of art does not entail its own risk. Not just in the way in which Plato has been tea-

... where grace is concerned, it is impossible for man to come anywhere near a puppet. Only a god can equal inanimate matter in this respect.

Grace appears most purely in that human form which either has no consciousness or an infinite consciousness. That is, in the puppet or in the god ...

— Heinrich von Kleist

To listen —
to open oneself, yourself, to the possibility of another;
to the possibility of being in communication with another;
an other that might be completely other not just to one, but to itself.
Where the otherness of another is perhaps what keeps this communion from being a consumption.

Connected
yet always separated;
separated only insofar that it is connected.
Keeping in mind that — *it is space that is first required to touch.* (Jean-Luc Nancy)

ching us: that one might not always like what the *daemon* whispers to us, into us; that the possibilities, thoughts, which are quite possibly opened in, within, us, might bring us to an unfamiliar place, one which possibility alters us. But that this very change, unfamiliarity, alteration, might well have always already been within, in, us;
in-potentiality.

For, a space — a dash — gives one space.
Which opens the possibility of touching. Yet, at the same time, allows for a run-up, opens the possibility of velocity — of the touch being a dashing. Where one might well be ruptured.

Dashed.

Which opens the question:
if one listens, tries to listen, does it, does the sound — what one considers, perhaps even calls, a sound — come from what, who, one attempts to listen to?, or, *is it a sound because one hears it, hears it as a sound?*

Perhaps, only because
one calls it a sound.

Which might well be the moment where *hearing ceases. Listening* as responding to, attending to, but always also potentially grasping, seizing upon ... *calling*.

[Here, you might want to pause and reflect on what your mother always told you: 'never go off with a stranger.' Perhaps what she neglected to tell you is that it is not just the — her, his — unfamiliarity that makes it potentially dangerous (in the sense that a different context — be it the person, place, or a combination of the two — causes you to act improperly) but more radically that the very strangeness that one encounters is quite possibilty from one's own self — that the impropriety might well be from within.]

For perhaps,
what is truly improper is one's continued attempt to dream of hope —
that one might actually be able to find a moment of, glimpse the possibility of, art.

Which is not to say that the phrase itself is erroneous:
after all, why must we read *dreams of hope* as an
affirmation,
a declaration — it can also, might well, be a question,
an empty claim, or even better, a plea ...
soft, weak, whimpering.

As long as art was making use of its own disappearance and the disappearance of its object, it still was a major enterprise. But art trying to recycle itself indefinitely by storming reality? The majority of contemporary art has attempted to do precisely that by confiscating banality, waste and mediocrity as values and ideologies. These countless installations and performances are merely compromising with the state of things, and with all the past forms of art history. Raising originality, banality and nullity to the level of values or even to perverse aesthetic pleasure. Of course, all of this mediocrity claims to transcend itself by moving art to a second, ironic level. But it is just as empty and insignificant on the second as on the first level. The passage to the aesthetic level salvages nothing; on the contrary, it is mediocrity squared. It claims to be null — "I am null! I am null! — and **it truly** is null.

For, it is precisely though its nullness that it seduces us;
by whispering ...
I can be whatever you want me to be

Which might mean that one's, your, hope lies in completely separating oneself from the art that one is attempting to respond to, perhaps even with. Where

The flip side of this duplicity is, through the bluff on nullity, to force people a contrario to give it all some importance and credit under the pretext that there is no way it could be so null, that it must be hiding something. Contemporary art makes use of this uncertainty, of the impossibility of grounding aesthetic value judgments and speculates on the guilt of those who

Call me
(call me)
on the line
Call me, call me
any, anytime
Call me
— Blondie

the with-ness, where bearing witness, lies in standing apart — not just to open the possibility of space, a gap, but precisely to maintain the gap, the space, between one and art itself.

do not understand it or who have not realized that there is nothing to understand. Another case of insider trading.

Independent art;
in the precise sense of keeping oneself apart from art.

Perhaps even *keeping one apart from the self's experience of art.*

II

To speak of the independence of some thing is to neglect its dependency. For, to speak of any thing is to open its relationality to another.

Which makes the term *indie art* a strange one —
and brings with it the question, *independent of what?*

Or: *independence from what?*

Certainly, one of the hopes of most artisans is for their work to be free from external pressures — most commonly, commerce. However, the fact that work is always already material suggests that it is linked with a certain exchangeability. For, even if the artisan did not pay for the said materials, the fact that they are now utilised for the work, and not for another purpose, suggests it has a use-value. And since, use and exchange-value are not quite — at least not completely — separable, the withdrawal of the materials from circulation suggests a certain cost; an opportunity cost, as it were.

However, even as this is an important consideration, this does not address the notion of art itself: for, this flattens the difference between *work* and *art*.

For, surely not everything an artisan produces can be considered art.

So, let's begin again, start anew

To begin to speak of indie art, one must first address the question: *what is art?*

A question haunted by another question, a dependent question: *is art art without the frame?* After all, sunflowers on a wall is graffiti; with(in) a frame it is — or at least is called — art. It only has a name — one might even say *it is called to its name* — within those walls.

Which opens another question: *is it only art when it has a name?* And, perhaps more importantly, *whose name?*: that of the work, or that of the one who signs on the work? Questions that we momentarily defer to consider: *where does the art lie?*

Perhaps in the presence of the original: for, who has not been genuinely moved by some work? But in this, the notion of names continues to be a spectre: for, *is it the name that lends the aura to the work?*

Would one be moved when standing in front of graffiti?

It is certainly possible: after all, no one questions the power of Banksy's work. However, the moment one knows — or even thinks that — it is a *Banksy,* the link between the work and the name remains.

A more interesting question is perhaps then: *can a replica have an aura?* For, if the aura lies in the work itself, there is no reason why a perfect replication — whether this is possible or not is another question — should not.

A particularly pertinent question in the digital age:
for, *is there an un-original code to begin with?*

However, there is little doubt that there is something different about an original: whether this is rational or not, or if it even has an explanation, is perhaps not quite the point.

For perhaps, the notion of originality itself lies in it being called, named, as original.

In its being authored as an origin (*auctor*).

Which opens the possibility that the originality of a work — the origin of a work — comes not so much from within but from elsewhere, from another. And here, we should keep in mind that both *elsewhere* and *from another* are positions of relation — and, more importantly — are in themselves unknown, potentially unknowable, locations.

And perhaps, it is precisely the *unlocatability* of art that has to be considered. Which opens a new register in the relationality between art and independence. For, if art is unlocatable, then surely it is always already independent: that would make the phrase *indie art*, tautological.

And, if unlocatable — and its aura can only be glimpsed as we stand before it — this suggests that the experience of art is singular.

And, as we cannot account for the origin of this aura, we can never know when we are in the presence of art until it affects us. After all, Plato teaches us that for craft to move into the realm of — to transcend itself to become — art, the artisan needs a divine moment; needs to be affected by a whisper from the *daemon*. But, since this is a moment that comes from beyond, this suggests that it is exterior to the artisan's knowledge, self, perhaps even being: a moment in which (s)he might well know naught what (s)he is doing.

Perhaps then, in order to experience art, we might need that moment too; in which we see a work with new eyes.

And this might well be the very crux of *indie art:*
that it is not so much that the art — or even the work — is independent from anything,

but that the independence is of the one — (s)he — who is looking ...

... from her very self.

III

... by representing things to ourselves, by naming them and conceptualizing them, human beings call them into existence, and at the same time hasten their doom ...

Writing Death

For, if in authoring a work we inevitably call its origin — no matter how imaginary — into being, then perhaps what we must do is the impossible: *separate the writing from the one who writes;*
separate the author from writing itself.

Or, even more radically: in writing, *write the death of the one who writes.*

Naming one — oneself — as writer as, at the very point when, one writes. Keeping in mind that the only time

Naming is a kind of calling, in the original sense of demanding and commending. It is not that the call has its being in the name; rather every name is a kind of call.
— Martin Heidegger

... ellipsis is the rhetorical equivalent of writing: it depletes, or decompletes, the whole so as to make conceptual totalities possible. And yet every conceivable whole achieved on the basis of ellipsis is stamped with the mark of the original loss. Like writing, it withdraws from the alternatives of presence and absence, whole and part, proper and foreign, because only on its ever eroding foundation can conceptual oppositions develop: it withdraws from its own concept. Ellipsis eclipses (itself). It is the 'figure' of figuration: the area no figure contains ...
— Werner Hamacher

in which one has to use a name is in the absence of the one who is named thus.

And in naming oneself as the one who writes, as the writer, all that one is doing is preparing for the absence of the one who is writing; perhaps all one is doing, in the very act of naming, is to begin mourning the day when there is nothing one can do but say, write, the name —

writer.

Perhaps then, to call it, name it — art — is to prepare for its absence, for the death of art.

However, to refuse to do so, to attempt to stave off its finitude, to hold its disappearance in abeyance, by refusing to name it, refusing it its name, is to turn down its call — to ignore it. Quite possibily to efface it: to deny any possibility of art itself.

And when faced with this
— effacement or death —
the choice between two of
the same,
what else can one do but
chuckle;
laugh.

... removing meaning brings out the essential point: namely, that the image is more important than what it speaks about — just as language is more important than what it signifies ... But it must also remain alien to itself in some way. Not reflect [on] itself as

medium, not take itself for an image. It must remain a fiction, a fable and hence echo the irresolvable fiction of the event …

An event is characterized entirely, in a paradoxical way, by its uncanniness, its troubling strangeness — it is the irruption of something improbable and impossible — and by its troubling familiarity: from the outset it seems totally self-explanatory, as through predestined, as though it could not but take place.

And what can be more elliptical, fragmentary, outside of reason — fragmenting even — than laughter?

Laughter as a question that remains a question; that opens a question that retains its radicality as question — and its impact on the, in the, imagination.

For, one either recognises — responds — to a joke or not: a joke can never be

The absolute rule, that of symbolic exchange, is to return what you received. Never less, but always more. The absolute rule of

explained; the moment it is brought back under reason, the joke is over.

And in this world where reality sutures every possible event into itself, into its own integral reality, all we can do is laugh—not at, not even with, but just laugh.

And that is its own event.

thought is to return the world as we received it: unintelligible. And if it is possible, to return it a little bit more unintelligible. A little bit more enigmatic.

The smile of the Cheshire cat; where all there is, is the smile ...

hopeless dreams

...

A version of this piece was commissioned by Jonathan Leong (ZXEROKOOL) for his group show, entitled *The Phygital World,* at the Chan Hampe Galleries Singapore, from 27 Nov–07 Dec 2014. All lines in pink are from Jean Baudrillard—to whom this chapter is dedicated.

I would like to begin right away by excusing myself because I know very little of what I am about to attempt to write on, very little of what I write.

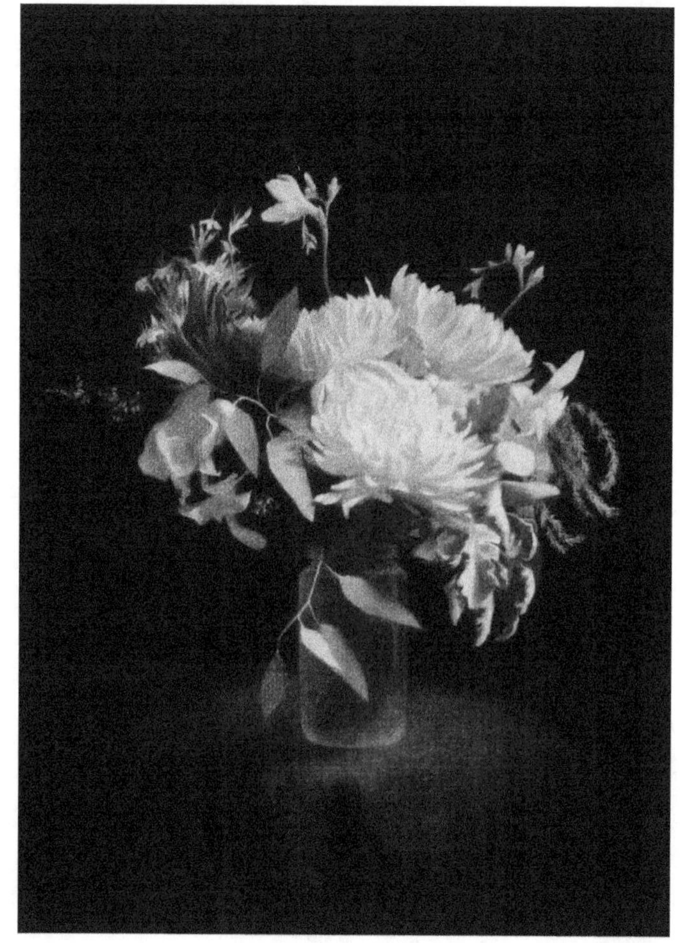

Flowers II, Nitram Charcoal on Fabriano Roma paper, 2014, 66cm by 82cm

Perhaps an excuse that comes a little too late. After all, I have already begun, at least in terms of words, scribbles, marks. Not that we can quite know when we ever actually begin.

Or, where a line even starts.

Perhaps then, I should have begun by asking to begin again. For, one might have already begun at the, in the very, moment when one has — I had — agreed to write on, about, with, Yanyun Chen's drawings. Which brings with it — opens — the question of whether one begins when, whilst, looking at her drawings. Or, if the manner, way, in which I am looking at them draws from the fact that I am going to write on them; if my looking is already infected by the writing that is to come; if I have already written on them even as I look, am looking, am about to look. If my look is only happening as I am drawn to the — her — drawings.

And where the first scribble might well have begun in the line between the looking and the object that is looked at. Where the scribble, the writing of this piece, had perhaps already begun at the point in which the drawing was being considered, thought about; had begun to write itself even as whether there would have been a drawing was being contemplated, when the sketch itself has yet to happen.

Where, what is being written is being written in blindness: not just to the sketches, to the drawings, but to its very self as writing. Not just because all sketching is made in blindness — for, the one who draws can only be looking at either the object or her drawing — and where all drawings are, as Jacques Derrida reminds us, memories of the blind, memoirs to blindness, memoirs of the blind. Not just because all writing is itself a scratching (*scribere*), a potential marking, tearing away, even as it is attempting to remark upon. But that writing upon, about, on, always already potentially writes over, overwrites; where what is written might have nothing to do with what is written on.

Where the sketch is drawn over, as it were.

Not by the one who writes, not even by the one who sketches, who draws, but by the very sketch — the very possibility of sketching — itself.

Which is not to say that the sketch cannot be seen. But that even as it — the drawing — is before one, before me, it is always already also written into. Where what is seen might well be the coming together of the sketch and its writing; the writing on it, from it — the two perhaps remaining indistinguishable.

And where this writing that you are reading is but the remainder; what is left over after the sketch has been seen, after you have been drawn into the drawing itself.

Which suggests that I both cannot write — for the writing has already happened — but must write — for the sketch continues, the sketches continue, to draw me — at the same time. Perhaps then a writing that, at best, happens through me: which is not a disavowal of responsibility — far from it. For, there is also no writing if I don't open myself to the possibility of it, *to writing writing itself through me.*

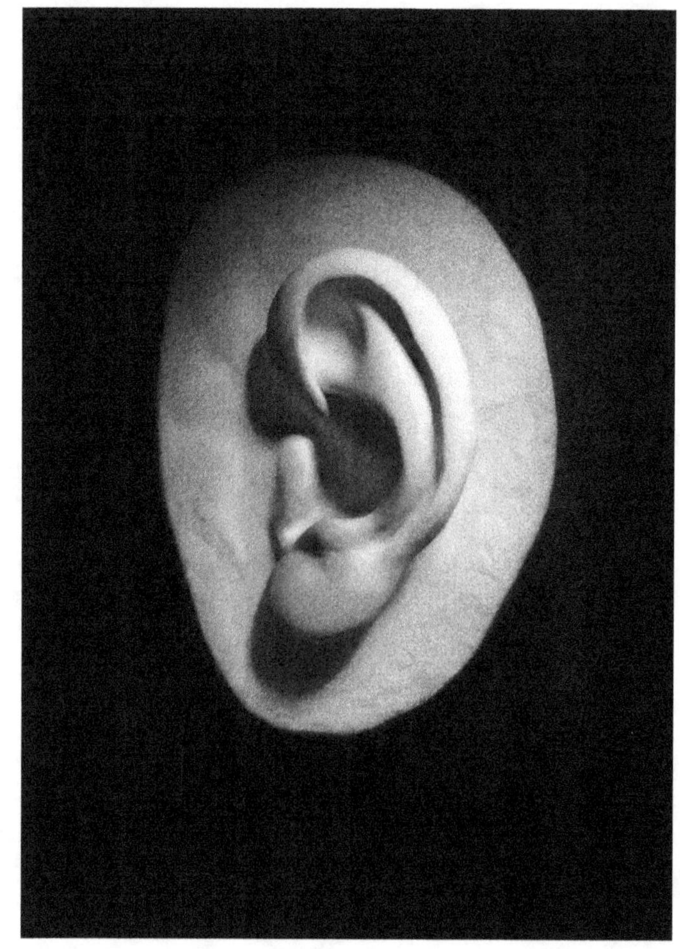

Ear Cast Drawing, Nitram Charcoal on Fabriano Roma paper, 2013

Write, let no one hold you back, let nothing stop you: not man, not the imbecilic capitalist machinery, in which publishing houses are the crafty, obsequious relayers of imperatives handed down by an economy that works against us and off our backs; and not yourself. Smug-faced readers, managing editors, and big bosses don't like the true texts of women — female-sexed texts. That kind scares them ...

— Hélène Cixous

A line
A line that lines
surrounds, borders.

Some call it a frame.
Keeping in mind that to frame not only entails what is
brought in, brought together, drawn into;
not only what is left out, excluded, exorcised, exiled;
not only what is left on the border, in the in-between, un-
wanted yet not free, *sans*
papiers;
but that to be framed also
entails being accused of
something that one has
not — or, at least, might not
have — done.

What Manet did [it is in any case one of the important aspects, I believe, of the changes contributed by Manet to western painting] was to make reappear, in a way, at the very interior of what was represented in the picture, these properties, these qualities or these material limitations of the canvas which painting, which the pictorial tradition, had up until then made its mission in some way to sidestep and to mask.

— Michel Foucault

Whether or not Manet did it is another question.

One that remains perhaps unanswerable.

At best, we can attempt to make his works, his paintings, testify for — perhaps against — him.
Perhaps then, an altogether
irrelevant question.

Which does not mean that one ceases, we cease, to continue the quest to attempt to discover something about his paintings, his work, something about him.

But perhaps, always already only something about Manet: Éduoard might well remain hidden from us, there but not quite there. In the *white shadows,* as it were.

And in that very spirit: if Manet is the one who "reinvents [or perhaps he invents] the picture-object, the picture as materiality, the picture as something coloured which clarifies an external light and in front of which, or about which, the viewer revolves," does Yanyun Chen invent [or, taking framing itself to its limits, I shall then say, *Yanyun Chen is the one who invents*] — although as one who knows very little of what I am writing about, who am I to say; so I shall say even though I have no right to — *the object-picture*;

the picture that objects to itself being a picture,
being depictured.

Not so much — or perhaps not just — the "reinsertion of the materiality of the canvas in that which is represented," but the rejection of that which is represented to being presented.

A rejection which she has long realised, felt at least. For, even as she has sketched these objects, drawn them, she has never quite acknowledged her drawing, her role in them. Where amidst all the marks of, on, the object, her mark, the mark of her, her name — *Yanyun Chen* — remains invisible.

Which is not to say that she is missing. For, just because her name remains veiled from us, from one, does not mean that it is not there — does not mean it does not remain to haunt us.

For, one should try not to forget that forgetting happens to one — one has no control over what one forgets, over forgetting itself. Which means that there is no way to know, of knowing, if every moment of remembering, every act of memory, brings with it forgetting — that forgetting is potentially part of memory itself.

Yanyun Chen
— a name we forgot —
the name of a forgotten.

Perhaps,
a name for forgetting itself.

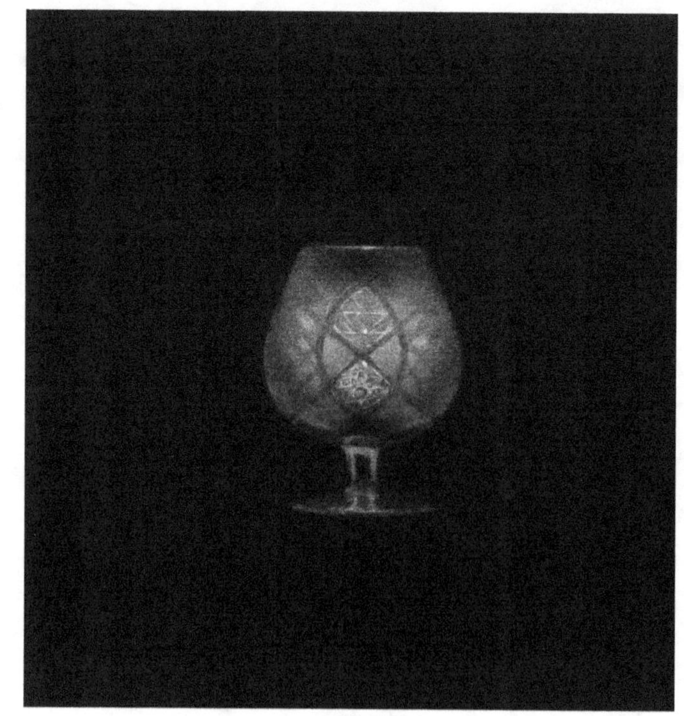

Crystal II, Nitram Charcoal on Fabriano Roma paper, 2014, 42cm by 42 cm

Forget meaning
and with it the subject ...
Beauty will be amnesiac or will not
be at all.

— Sylvère Lotringer

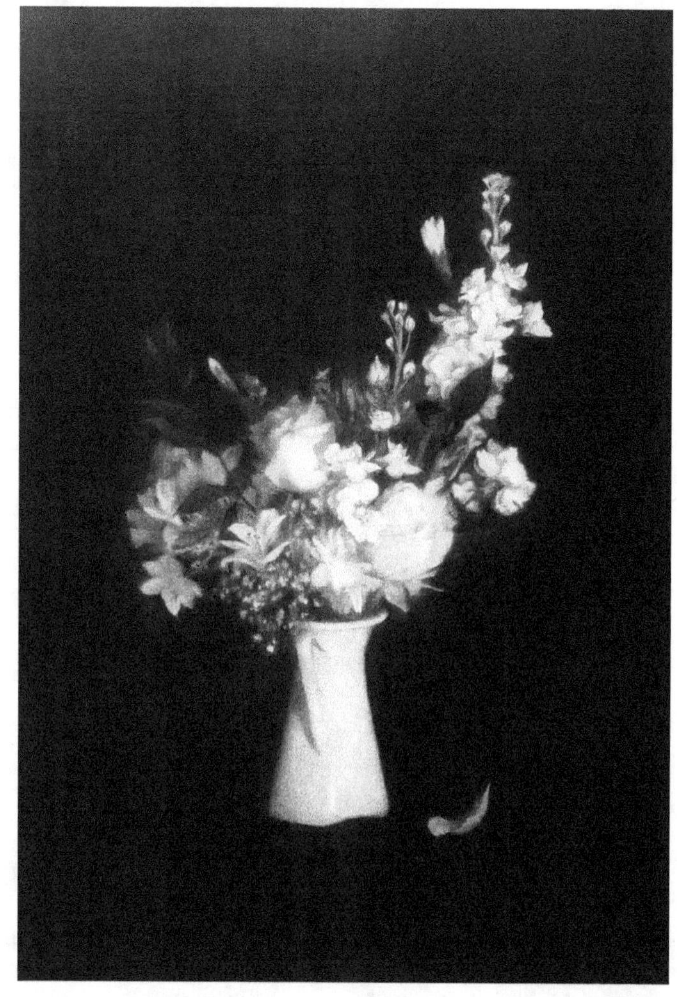

Dorian Gray, site specific installation, *Destruction and Rebirth*, The Mill, Singapore.

Along with the poet Novalis, who died much too young, I am of the opinion that the sciences belong to the poetized and that they should be handled musically, because musical relations appear to be the 'fundamental relations of Nature'. But, I do not share with Novalis the despairing search for the absolute in all things. I try to substitute this search with a method of fortuitous finds ...

— Siegfried Zielinski

Discovery and possibilities. The possibilities in discovery. The very discovery as a possibility in itself. Not one that looks for something, but stumbles upon, perhaps blindly — stumbling around in the dark — and in that blind moment, quite possibly also sees.

Groping, reaching about ...

... attending to the echoes
between things, persons,
ideas.

Listening out for thoughts calling to each other.
Attuning oneself, opening one's registers to possibilities that have yet to be heard.

Opening possibility by listening to
the possibility of music.
Poetry.

And whenever we hear of poetry, Plato's warning of its danger, its dangers, is never far away. After all, at its highest levels, poetry echoes the whispers of the *daemon*, potentially rendering all our defences — reason, rationality — against the onslaught of *pathos* useless; perhaps leading one away from being a good person. But, who ever said that embarking on a journey, uncovering, unveiling, was safe. For, one might find out that one does not like what one finds.

Like Pandora.

For, even gifted ones aren't immune from the inherent dangers in gifts.

And when we speak of gifts, the echo of data is never far away.

Here, it might be prudent to tune our registers to the note of *datum* that resounds in data; a giving where the parties involved are of an unequal standing. Thus, without any expected, or even possible, reciprocation of this gift. As opposed to *munus*; an exchangeable gift, a gift of relation between two or more parties. In this exchange, a symbol is shared between the parties — a *symbolum* (creed, mark), is broken; after which all parties keep a part of it. And where the exchange of the gift itself is crucial — the actual object is somewhat arbitrary, but there has to be an object. But since *datum* entails unexchangeability, this suggests that it can also be objectless; where the gift is in the giving. Thus, the manner in which it is received is equally important. For, if its status as a gift is in its giving, it is only a gift when recognised: its very status depends on the response, on there being a response.

Thus, what is exchanged between the one who gives and the one who receives is nothing other than time itself.

The time taken to see.

To look.

To let oneself be open to the work.

To respond to the call of the work.

The time taken to recognise the possibility of the work as gift: a gift that gives itself even as the object refuses to be presented. The work that is an objectless work: a work that gives itself as one attempts to respond to, with, it.

As Yanyun Chen attempts to respond with the object—even as the object resists her.

Where, at the point of being sketched, the object perhaps utters, "I am for you what you want me to be at the moment you look at me in a way you've never seen me before: at every instant." (Cixous) A sketching that foregrounds

sketch
a 'rough drawing intended to serve as the basis for a finished picture'; from *schets* (Dutch) or *skizze* (Low German); both apparently 17c. artists' borrowings from *schizzo* (Italian), 'sketch, drawing'; which is commonly said to be from *schedius* (Latin).

a response to the object that cannot — does not pretend to — see the object itself. Which represents — for this is inevitable; after all, one is drawing something — which presents, but which does not claim to present the object that one is sketching. That, at most, is a sketchy version of the form (*skhēma*) of the object — one that might well be temporary, extemporaneous, made off-hand (*skhedios*).

The OED compares *schedius* to *schedia* (raft) & *schedium* (an extemporaneous poem); from or related to *skhedios* (Greek), 'temporary, extemporaneous, done or made off-hand'; which is related to *skhēma* (form, shape, appearance).

" ... a method of fortuitous finds ..." (Zielenski)

Much like when I attempt to write about her sketchings.

For, "when I write, it's everything that we don't know we can be that is written out of me, without exclusions, without stipulation, and everything we will be calls us to the unflagging, intoxicating, unappeasable search for love." (Cixous)

Keeping in mind that the dossier of love brings with it the question of: is one responding to the *what*, the characteristics of the thing, the person; or the who, the person, thing, as such. Which is not to say that *what* and *who* are necessarily distinguishable, separable, to begin with. However, if we open the register that the *who* is always already beyond us — outside of knowability, even if only slightly — this suggests that it is the spectre, the potentially unknowable, which haunts all relationality.

Thus, even if there is an object to one's love — without which one cannot even begin to speak of love, speak of response, of relation — this might well be an objectless object or, at least, an object that remains veiled from us.

Perhaps then, the time taken to attempt to respond — through sketching, drawing, writing — might well be also the time for the work to draw one into it, sketch itself into one.

Where perhaps *the time of the drawing* is nothing other than *the drawing of time itself.*
Not that we might ever be able to know it.

For, all we ever can see — Yanyun Chen's drawings, sketches; my writing — are its shadows.

That is, if white ink even casts any.

Jusqu'au bout.

...

This piece is inspired by, dedicated to, Yanyun Chen and her sketchings.

CONTENTS

ABOUT THE CONTRIBUTORS

Jeremy Fernando is the Jean Baudrillard Fellow at the European Graduate School, where he is also a Reader in Contemporary Literature & Thought. He works in the intersections of literature, philosophy, and the media; and has written eleven books — including *Reading Blindly, Living with Art,* and *Writing Death.* His work has also been featured in magazines and journals such as *Berfrois, CTheory, TimeOut,* and *VICE*; and he has been translated into Spanish and Slovenian. Exploring other media has led him to film, music, and art; and his work has been exhibited in Seoul, Vienna, Hong Kong, and Singapore. He is the general editor of both Delere Press and the thematic magazine *One Imperative*; and a Fellow of Tembusu College at the National University of Singapore.

Alessandro De Francesco is a poet, artist, and essayist based in Basel and Brussels. PhD at the Sorbonne, Visiting Faculty at the European Graduate School, and formerly director of the poetry atelier at the École Normale Supérieure in Paris, he is the author of numerous publications in several languages and has performed and exhibited worldwide.

www.ingramcontent.com/pod-product-compliance
Lightning Source LLC
LaVergne TN
LVHW020511100826
845148LV00003B/760

* 9 7 8 9 4 9 1 9 1 4 0 5 8 *